The River Ba at Killiechronan looking back towards Beinn Ghraig (near Gruline)

LEFT: The 13th century nunnery, Iona   RIGHT: Loch Peallach on the Tobermory – Dervaig road

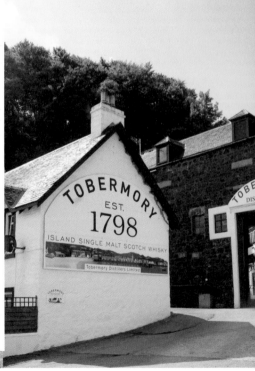

LEFT: Ulva Ferry   RIGHT: Tobermory Distillery

Mull and Iona

Mull has all the benefits of an island and the comfort of being 7 miles/11 km from Oban on the Scottish mainland of Argyllshire. It is 46 minutes by CalMac ferry and only 18 minutes from Lochaline across the Sound of Mull to Fishnish, between Salen and Craignure. It is 29 miles in length and 30 miles in breadth (approx. 50 km) in each direction. At 353 sq. miles/875 sq km, it is the largest of the Inner Hebridean Islands after Skye. The population is c. 2,800 (1901: 4,334).

Mull adjoins the Sound of Mull to the north and the Firth of Lorne to the east. The coastline extends to some 300 miles. It is rugged and irregular, spectacularly beautiful, with many small islands, especially in the west. The most well known are Iona and Staffa, with Ulva the largest, situated very close to Gometra and with several other groupings of islands scattered about. Iona lies at the southern tip of Mull, the object of pilgrims in three millennia, the place where Columba landed in AD 563. Staffa is well known for Fingal's Cave, the largest of several caves there, particularly because of its columnar basalt formations and Mendelssohn.

The highest mountains are in the south east. Mull boasts one Munroe, Ben More, rising to 3,169 ft/866m, but its mountainous scenery is none-the-less dramatic, matching the exceptionally picturesque south coastline facing (for the most part) the islands of Ulva and Gometra. South west of Tobermory is Calgary Bay, noted for its acres of flat, soft white sand, surrounded by cliffs and high moorland; unspoilt, uncrowded (because of its size) and undeveloped: a jewel in Mull's crown.

Mull is great; a place for an island hideaway holiday. A place where the pace is slower and quieter. Mobile phone signals can be poor or not available. At the time of writing, don't bank on BT phone boxes working either. Mull enjoys a particularly good reputation for its wildlife. It is a very important part of the island economy now. Watching wildlife here is so easy. Whether on a tour (land or sea based) – from whales, dolphins, the occasional orca and numerous seals to the inquisitive otter, the eagles of course, or just a lonely heron, strutting along the shoreline for its next meal. Then there are the deer grazing in quiet locations and not to be forgotten, the array of other birds that make Mull their home.

Mull maintains your interest with a mixture of high mountains, moorland and forest and low tree/shrub cover, broken by pastures for grazing sheep (and some cattle) and heath land with many burns (streams) rushing down to the sea. The Tourist Information describes Mull as having a coast line of unending beauty. It is an apt description. With its network of only single track roads, exploring has to be done at a slow speed: safety demands it. Mull is therefore a place where you can unwind, explore and become captivated by the island's attractiveness.

Getting There

CalMac operate ferries from Oban – Craignure; Lochaline – Fishnish; Kilchoan – Tobermory (all sailing the Sound of Mull), plus Fionnphort to Iona.[Contact: Oban Terminal/Office: ☎ 01631 566688 (daily 8.30 – 1800). General Enquiries: ☎ 0800 066 5000, www:calmac.co.uk for on-line bookings].

For cheaper return tickets avoid Saturday if possible, they are now available for up to nine days. Sailings from Oban – Craignure on a Saturday are more expensive except some early/late departures, therefore look for accommodation which suits this arrangement if possible. Also, book early and on line for saver deals.

On arrival in Oban, if you are not already booked, park in the lane assigned for those without tickets. Then go to the booking office without delay. Check-in closes 30 minutes before sailing for vehicles and 10 minutes for foot passengers. Pedal cycles go free, as do children under 5 years of age.

The Oban – Craignure ferry is a large vessel and has restaurant/bar facilities. Look out for Duart Castle perched on a rocky outcrop a few minutes before reaching Craignure. It is the home of the chief of the Clan Maclean and dates from the 13th century. As you leave Oban, the island on your left is Kerrera in the Firth of Lorn. The one (later on) on your right with the lighthouse is Lismore in Loch Linnhe.

Driving on Mull: Important!

Other than sections of the A849 / A848 between the Craignure area and Tobermory, the rest of the island network consists of single track roads with (usually) frequent laybys. The rule of the road is give way to the vehicle coming towards you and also, pull in to allow a faster vehicle behind you to pass. Drive slowly: you will meet vehicles on blind bends. Remember that many road side verges are soft. You will see more of the spectacular scenery if you are taking your time. On a busy day, the Iona road will see you making frequent pull-ins. The return journey is less demanding in the early evening if you can plan it that way.

Do not cross the road to use a layby. You are advised to avoid running low on petrol/diesel. There are filling stations on Tobermory quay, Salen, and Craignure and just inland from Fionnphort.

It is worth noting that if you are heading for the Dervaig area and are at Salen (or the other way around), there is a useful short cut from Aros, 1.5miles/2.5km west of Salen on the Tobermory road. It cuts up Glen Aros and although it runs through tracts of forest, it is generally quite scenic and quiet. It reaches Dervaig by its church and unusual round tower.

The Lochaline – Fishnish Ferry

From the Ballachulish – Fort William road (A82), you need to cross Loch Linnhe on the Corran ferry to Ardgour. It only takes a few minutes to cross over. It is one of the last mainland ferries in Scotland. The A861 from Corran is a two lane road running down a deep valley of mixed woodland, crossing from the north side to the south after12miles/20km upon reaching the head of Loch Sunart. The A884, a single track road, then takes you on to Lochaline. After 4 miles/6km, it rises away from Loch Sunart, heading south. The total distance from the Corran ferry to Lochaline is 31 miles/51km.

There are panoramic views down a pronounced glen towards Ben More on Mull as you head south. As the road descends (about 6miles/10km from Lochaline), you reach an area of mixed deciduous woodland, but predominantly oak – at least by the road, which creates a pleasant run down to the ferry. Ardtornish House gardens are passed near to Lochaline. There are a snack bar and toilets at the ferry terminal. Lochaline has the Whitehouse Restaurant, a recent Highlands and Islands Restaurant of the Year. [Contact: Lochaline, Morvern, PA34 5XT, ☎ 01967 421777]

A kayak route along the Ardtornish Estate coastline was ranked by National Geographic's Traveler Magazine as one of the 50 greatest tours of the world. The estate is the home to the native cat and the pine marten. This large estate offers holiday accommodation. [Contact: Ardtornish Estate Office, Morvern, Oban, Argyll, PA80 5UZ, e: stay@ardtornish.co.uk]. There is a lot to see in the extensive gardens which are open throughout the year, with impressive colours and range of plants, trees etc. Garden entrance 2 miles/3km before Lochaline.

Craignure

This small community huddles against the A849 coast road. It goes to the left for Duart Castle and Iona, right for Salen and Tobermory. Opposite the jetty are CalMac's offices, tourist information and the Spar shop. There is a small car park behind the toilets. To the left is the popular Craignure Inn, an old drovers' inn, now with a good name for its food. Almost opposite, behind the community hall is a well appointed caravan/camp site with views out to sea plus good facilities, including a common room building. Within half a mile to the west (to the right on leaving the jetty) is a large hotel/spa complex, the Isle of Mull Hotel. Craignure also has a golf course, but if you remember the narrow guage railway and Torosay Castle from a previous visit, they are now closed.

Taking the Tobermory road, there are plenty of views to the coast and across the Sound to the Morven peninsula. After a couple of miles, a right turn heads down to Fishnish and the ferry to Lochaline. Continuing on for a couple of miles or so you pass Pennygown, with its ruined chapel, before reaching Salen. This compact community sits at the junction of the Tobermory road and a left turn to Gruline, a 3 mile/5km link road to Loch Na Keal and the south /south west side of the island.

Salem has a hotel and other accommodation, a Spar grocery shop, filling station, car and bike repairs, restaurants and Post Office. The road this far is backed by mountainous countryside and Glen Forsa (visible between the trees from near the Glen Forsa Hotel). It is a deep and significant glen (valley) cutting through to the Craignure – Iona road but alas not with a modern roadway to afford a short cut!

Leaving Salen for Tobermory, the A848 hugs Salen Bay for a little over a mile before turning left along the short estuary of the Aros River. Across the water are the scant remains of the 13th century Aros Castle. At the head of the inlet is the turn for the road up Glen Aros, which offers a direct route to Dervaig c. 10 miles/16 km away (the B8073). From here, the A848 climbs up and away from the coast, but the views are stunning (perhaps at their best on the return trip to Salen) out to the Sound of Mull and across it to Morvern.

Tobermory

The only town on the island, Tobermory sits at the head of a bay sheltered by the small Calve Island. In 1773, Dr Johnson found 12-14 sailing ships here but learnt that on another day, he might have seen 60 or so. It had an inn but probably not many houses. He ate there on bread and butter, then a dish in its own right, both of course being homemade. Today it is a thriving community, its trade augmented by many visitors. Many children must have grown up thinking that this is Balamory from the Childrens' TV programmes. Its distinctly painted buildings add colour and vibrancy to the waterfront.

With a new Marine Visitor Centre on the quayside just beyond the distillery, a theatre, good accommodation and restaurants, Co-op, a diversion to the distillery etc there is much to do and see here. If the Marine Visitor Centre aquaints you with life beneath the waves, the Museum brings Tobermory's heritage to life. Both useful places to occupy time on a wet day or whet your curiosity.

ABOVE: Tobermory

BELOW: Fishing and pleasure boats at the quay, Tobermory

Upon arrival, just outside the town there is the Mull Theatre [Contact: at Druimfin, Tel: 01688 302828] on your right and a small shopping outlet on your left. Here is the Mull Pottery, smoked fish/seafood, a gift shop, gallery and café. Descending downhill into Main Street and the waterfront, a right turn by the distillery of 1798 puts you onto the Ledaig Quay. Other than whisky, there is a filling station, motor garage, pub and food, outdoor clothes shop, the Marine Visitor Centre (including toilets), tourist information, car park and boating facilities, beyond the car park.

The waterfront has a wide range of shops: a soap shop and chocolate shop where you can indulge yourself for a while, various craft shops, the Mull Pottery outlet, Co-op, bank (and ATM tucked around the side) a pharmacy [Contact: ☎ 01688 302431], Post Office, places to eat and stay, book a wildlife cruise etc. The Museum is here too but it is only open Easter – October, Mon-Fri, other times by appointment only. There is on street parking, the old jetty to wander along where the fishing boats tie up and at the far end, the ferry across the Sound to Kilchoan on the Ardnamurchan peninsula. This is a 35 minute sailing all year round Mon-Sat and Sundays between May- Aug. This ferry awaits the arrival of the bus from Craignure if you advise the ferry office there no later than 4pm on the day of travel. ☎ 01680 812343 and ensure you choose Option 2.

Exploring Tobermory

The information centre next to the Marine Visitor Centre can help with your enquiries [Contact: ☎ 01688 302875/301268]. Much of Tobermory exists from the late 18th century when the British Fisheries Association bought the area off the Duke of Argyll to establish an alternative way of life for impoverished crofters. It was not the success it was intended to be. It was tourism, encouraged through railways on the mainland which brought growth in the Highland and Island economies. A visit by Queen Victoria on the Royal Yacht also encouraged visitors and its sheltered harbour and bay was an important asset. It still is.

The Marine Visitor Centre

This innovative and really interesting attraction opened in 2012. It portrays life in a working harbour and in the sea beyond, with informative and interactive displays. It is an absorbing place to visit and learn much about Tobermory and the sea. There is a touch pool for children (the exhibits are returned to the sea) and a small cinema. Open all the year round, this is great to visit anytime and invaluable in bad weather, especially with children. It is run by the Tobermory Harbour Association. There are toilets here (nice and clean) with a small charge to further the centre's activities.

ABOVE: The (Harbour) Marine Visitor Centre

BELOW: Aros Castle, Aros Mains

Mull Museum

Situated on the waterfront in Main Street, this museum presents artifacts and memorabilia of Mull's history in themed displays. These include a blackhouse, the ancient Hebridean dwelling house; a shipwrecked Spanish galleon; bygone working tools of craftsmen from years ago; and World War II action at Tobermory. It is open Easter-end of October [contact: www.mullmuseum.org.uk]

Aros Park

This is the large area of parkland formerly attached to the demolished Aros House and may be reached off the Salen road (a half mile out of Tobermory) or by a footpath from the Ledaig car park next to MacGochan's pub. Entrance is free. Forestry Commission Scotland provide parking, barbecue facilities, toilets and several paths with disabled access. Calve Island, which stretches across the entrance to the bay at Tobermory can be reached at low tide for a short time only along a sand bank from the park. **Remember to leave adequate time to get back**. It was used to drive cattle to and from the island in former times.

Tobermory Golf Club: ☎ 01688 302741, e:secretary@tobermorygolfclub.com
Youth Hostel: on the quay side, in one of the town's brightly painted buildings, ☎ 01688 302481, e: tobermory@syha.org.uk

Eating Out In Tobermory

For something a little different:

An Tobar Café: situated in Tobermory's Art Centre. Housed in a former Victorian School. ☎ 01688 302211
Tobermory Hotel: Waterfront dining in Main Street. ☎ 01688 302091
Mull Pottery: Café/Bistro situated above the Mull Pottery shop/gallery, just outside of town on the road to Salen. ☎ 01688 302347
Glengorm Coffee Shop: Situated below an art gallery displaying work by local artists. Sells a range of food as well as coffee! Farm shop adjacent and situated at Glengorm Castle, 4 miles/ 6 km north west of Tobermory. ☎ 01688 302321. Open: March – October. The castle is not open to the public.

Calgary Beach / Photo: Chris Askew

Beaches

Mull has many miles of untouched coastline, much of it accessible/or visible off the coast roads that hug the sea at Loch Tuath, opposite Ulva; the road that follows Loch Na Keal south west of Gruline; and the coastal stretches of the road from Salen to Iona alongside Loch Scridain. There are of course coastal stretches of the road along the Sound of Mull running south east of Tobermory too. Elsewhere, the coastline is more difficult to reach, such as on the south side of the Ross of Mull and the coast facing eastwards to the mainland. Here the number of access roads are few and not many run along the coast (none for any distance).

If you do decide to stop at a quiet spot on the shoreline, remember not to block the single lane road at all.

Most of the beaches are small and rocky, but Mull does have a few good sandy beaches, including one or two really good ones. Probably the best of all is **Calgary beach**, about 13 miles/21 km from Tobermory, beyond Dervaig on the B8073. Here a sheltered bay is covered by a large expanse of white sand. A shallow river cuts through it and it is truly idyllic. Short stay wild camping is permitted, but no caravans or mobile homes. There are toilets and a car park. This safe, unspoilt beach is just great and large enough to accommodate day visitors and a host of campers.

North of the Calgary – Dervaig road are two more particularly good beaches. About 1.75 miles/3 km from Calgary bay is **Langamull beach** with a car park at Grid Ref NM 395520. It is a Forestry car park just off the B8073, with a couple of miles of walking involved. [Bus 494 from Tobermory]. Initially, the track runs through forest and then along the edge of it before leaving it behind to reach the sea.

Port Na Ba beach is a little to the right of Langamull (facing the sea). On leaving Dervaig for Calgary, the B8073 climbs uphill to pass the strikingly designed Am Birlinn restaurant on the left. Just past this is a turn to the right to Croig beach. The road ends here, but a path goes left towards the headland. Just before it, Port Na Ba beach on the right. It means Bay of the Cattle and was where cattle were driven ashore having been brought over from the Small Islands offshore in days gone by.

On the south side of the island are another five good bays. Two of these have road access, all be it well off the beaten track, and another near one of these with a road within half a mile. The easterly one is **Laggan Sands** at Lochbuie From Craignure, take the A849 towards Fionnphort and Iona. After 15 miles/ 24km and having just past the Inverlussa Mussel farm, take the left turn to Lochbuie and Croggan. It is a further 8 miles /13 km to Lochbuie. The road runs though deciduous woodland (chiefly oak) and attractive scenery to Loch Spelve, running along the loch side and then down the side of land-locked Loch Uisg to reach Lochbuie and Loch Buie.

Upon reaching the loch side, you enter a vast area of rhododendron ponticum. It must look impressive when the purple flowers are in bloom and cover the mountain side, at other times it is an intrusive nuisance to many country lovers. After passing a sign to a stone circle, you reach your destination, with the former post office hut selling ice cream etc at the end of the road. Beyond the rocky fore shore there is a long sandy beach. It is heralded as one of the best beaches in Britain for wildlife spotting.

There is also a commemorative plaque erected in 1902, to mark the coronation of King Edward VII and Queen Alexandra, by 'Lochbuie (the 23rd Clan Chief: Murdoch Maclean) and the Highlanders'. Nearby is a 3-story tower, Moy Castle, built in the 15th century and standing on the edge of the fore shore.

The Ross of Mull has four good beaches. For two of them, take the road to the left, off the Iona road having climbed uphill out of Bunessan, to Uisken. Go past the right turn to Ardachy Hotel and descend to **Uisken Beach**. There are rocky outcrops in the bay, probably a few caravans but a large beach, plenty of peace and quiet and little else. Except that is in August, when the childrens' Beach Games Day is held here. For the adjacent **Ardalanish Beach**, take the right turn for the hotel and Ardalanish Weavers, where there is a car park and a half mile walk to the beach. There are no facilities. There is a large crescent shaped beach crossed by a stream. The Weavers are open to the public.

There are two beaches close to each other to the south of Fionnphort. **Fidden Beach** is the nearest. From the village, take the road left (south) at the Columba Centre to Fidden Farm, a distance of 1.25 miles/2 km, the farm being at a left hand turn in the road. There is access to the beach here and camping facilities. The Beach is a favourite spot for seals. There are no facilities.

If you continue along the lane to its end, you reach Knockvologan. Park at Knockvologan. It is a short walk to the beach, which at low tide, allows access to the relatively large island of Erraid. It is about one mile square and apparently was the inspiration for R.L. Stevenson's *'Kidnapped'*. **Allow time to return in safety.**

LEFT: Uisken RIGHT: Lochbuie ABOVE: Calgary Bay

On the B8035 from Salen to Gruline

Eorsa Island from Killiechronan Campsite

McQuarrie's Mausoleum

Sound of Ulva

Eas Fos Waterfall from Ulva Ferry

Unusual rock formations on Inch
Kenneth Island

The south coast of Calgary Bay

Eagle Watching and Wildlife Tours

Following the successful reintroduction of sea eagles to Rum, they re-established themselves on Mull, Ardnamurchan etc. They remain very rare and are carefully protected. It is illegal to approach the bird or its nest without a licence. An eagle hide has been established for the benefit of visitors and bird watchers. Booking may be made by telephoning ☎ 01680 812556. You are met at a predetermined point and taken to the hide, which is open from 10am-1 pm. It is wonderful to see these huge birds soaring across the sky or gliding down to the sea, tallons outstretched to close on an unsuspecting fish loitering just below the surface.

 The variety of the wildlife, both on the land and in the sea around the coast makes Mull a superb destination. Whether it be sea or golden eagles, whales, dolphins, the orca, seals, otters, plus red deer and many other others species, there is much to choose from. The location is subject to change.

There are several wildlife guides, tours including:

Discover Mull ☎ 01688 400415; e: tour@discovermull.co.uk

Isle of Mull Experience ☎ 01681 700375; e: tour@ isleofmullexperience.co uk

Isle of Mull Wildlife & Bird Safaries ☎ 01680 300441; e: richard@atkinsons6273.freeserve.co.uk

Isle of Mull Wildlife Expeditions ☎ 01688 500121; e: info@scotlandwildlife.com

Mull Magic ☎ 01688 301213/07923153976; e: enquiries@mullmagic.com

Turus Mara, wildlife and seabird cruise tours ☎ 01688 400242; e: info@turusmara.com

ABOVE: Otter on the beach / Photo: Chris Askew

Salen to Gruline, Ulva Ferry and on to Tobermory

This is a route of stunning scenery, most of it hugging the coast along Loch Na Keal with views to Eorsa and Inch Kenneth Islands, Ben More and beyond. It then follows Loch Tuath with views over to Ulva and Gometra before the road cuts over to Calgary Bay and Dervaig. It then climbs uphill and inland before descending down to Tobermory. The road is single track with passing places, so just take your time and enjoy the memorable views.

In Salen, the B8035 forms a T-junction with the A848 (the Tobermory road) and the A849 (Craignure road). Follow the B8035 towards Gruline. It climbs uphill before levelling off and running along the bottom of a range of hills to your left, which fall precipitously towards the road. They rise up to Cruach Torr an Lochain at 1,141ft /348m in height. Whatever the climatic conditions, this range, and others on Mull always seem to appear dramatic, but especially Ben More and its associated mountains a little further on which are about to come into view.

After 2.5miles/4.5km, the B8073 goes off to the right to the tiny hamlet of Killiechronan, with its pony trekking centre and camp site just beyond. Here the River Ba, which drains out of Loch Ba at the northeast foot of Ben More, disappears into an accumulation of sand and stones to reach the sea. This small campsite has a fantastic view down the loch to Eorsa Island, with mountains either side of Loch Na Keal contributing to the drama.

BELOW: Ulva and Ulva Sound

ABOVE: Loch Tuath

McQuarrie's Mausoleum

Before turning right for Ulva ferry; it is worth going on just a little further to a brown sign pointing the way to McQuarrie's Mausoleum. It is owned by the National Trust – of Australia (New South Wales) but maintained for them by Historic Scotland. Here rests the father of Australia, Lochlan McQuarrie, his second wife Elizabeth, and their children Lachlan and Jane. He was the military Governor of a penal colony, but whilst there, developed it into the first civil community and State of what became New South Wales. By the time that he returned to Britain – he was born on Ulva – he left behind the institutions of the new state and gave it its name: Australia. Unless you need vehicular access because of disability, you are requested to leave your car at the roadside and walk down the 500 yard (or so) drive. It passes through a private house garden but is well signposted. Keep to the drive, closing the three gates on the way to reach the mausoleum. It is in a lawned, stone walled enclosure, a simple stone built building with a ridged roof, but no internal access. McQuarrie spent his final years nearby. There is an interpretation board.

Returning to the B8073, the road runs along the coast for about 5 miles/8 km before rising up to cut across a small headland and dropping down to Ulva Ferry. The extra height improves the view across to the eastern end of Ulva, the Sound of Ulva and Inch Kenneth island over to your left with its strange rock formations at the southern end. To use the Ulva Ferry, follow the instructions on the white board on the jetty. The ferryman will see it and come across to pick you up. The restaurant over there has a good reputation. The ferry ride itself takes 2-3 minutes.

From the car park (toilets available here), look across the bay to Eas Fors, the large waterfall tumbling over the cliff edge and into the sea. Continuing along the coast, the island of Gometra becomes easier to see separated from Ulva by a narrow channel. You are now travelling along Loch Tuath, a wide sea loch of similar size to Loch Na Keal.

It is 4 miles /6 km from the turning to Ulva Ferry to Torloisk, where the hill road climbs away to the right, running due north to Dervaig. It is possibly the road used by Dr Johnson to get to Ulva. The coast road is wider however, if a little longer and it is more interesting. From the road junction it is a little over a mile to Kilninian's old church, just before the road starts to rise away from the coast. There are interesting and ancient tomb chests here, the church dating from the mid-18th century.

Having left the coast, the road turns northwards and cuts across little populated moorland with great views out to sea and north towards Skye. It drops down to Calgary Bay, described on page 11, the road clinging to the coast above the sea as it passes along the bay. A short distance from the head of this glorious bay and beach is a farmhouse with tea room and gallery: Calgary Art in Nature – exhibiting wooden sculpture in a woodland setting.

Leaving Calgary, the road climbs up onto the moorland and forestry which separates it from Dervaig. There are Forestry Commission picnic areas on the way. At Penmore, there is a striking new development on the right, the Am Birlinn Restaurant. [Contact: Penmore, PA75 6QS; Tel: 01688 400619. Reservations recommended for lunch, essential for evening. Closed Mon/ Tues.] Here too, but on the opposite side of the road, is the Discover Mull Wildlife Tours [Contact: see page 15].

Descending to Dervaig, there is a right turn to the Old Byre Heritage Centre, just before the village. [Contact: Dervaig, PA75 6QR; ☎ 01688 400229]. This is a worthwhile attraction, combining a museum of Mull's wildlife, a film show (on wildlife or history, depending upon the day), a childrens' play area and a tea room. Open: from 1st Sunday in April – last Friday in October, closed Mon /Tues].

Dervaig is perhaps better known for its distinctive and unusual church round tower, which is painted white. Although the church was originally built in 1755,

LEFT: The coast road near Gribun on Loch Na Keal   RIGHT: Inch Kenneth Island

LEFT: Loch Scridain RIGHT: Loch Scridain looking north towards Glen More

Duart Castle

LEFT: Craignure and jetty   RIGHT: The former Post Office at Lochbuie

ABOVE: The Southside of Loch Na Keal

BELOW: Pennyghael

it was replaced by the current building 150 years later. Dervaig is a planned village of 1799, the initial development consisting mainly of the 26 houses which line the main street, opposite the church. The Bellachroy Inn is a former drovers' inn for the drovers coming ashore nearby from the outlying islands with their cattle, sheep etc. The village has a Post Office and village shop.

From the church, the right turn takes you down Glen Aros directly to Aros, near to Salen.

The B8073 to Tobermory climbs out of the village ahead. Once on the top, there is a sign to the right to Loch Frisa, the longest and largest lake on Mull. There is a cycle/walkers' track on the north side, which runs down the Salen Forest close to the lake shore. There is no road for motorists however. The lake is 4.5miles/7km in length and has a maximum width of about a half mile. Motorists have to make do with the three lakes at the roadside before the road descends to Tobermory: Lochs Carnain an Amais, Meadhoin and Peallach. From here, it is a few minutes by car into town and the Ledaig car park on the waterfront.

Gruline to Loch Scridain and on to Iona

To reach Iona or the southern end of Mull (the Ross of Mull), there are two choices of route for the first section, thereafter just the one road from the head of Loch Scridain. Of the two, the Gruline route is the most scenic. It runs along the water's edge and beneath Ben More for c.10 miles/16 km from the junction with the Ulva Ferry road, through Gruline to Gribun, before turning inland. With a dramatic backdrop of mountains on your left, the view across Loch Na Keal over pebbly beaches is captivating. The road (B8035) is single track.

First, unoccupied Eorsa Island is passed, followed by Inch Kenneth Island, with Ulva behind it. Inch Kenneth has a long history of occupation, with Lord Redesdale buying it in the 1930s. Thereafter, for a while, it became a fashionable place to find yourself on the guest list either as his guest or of his daughters, the Mitford sisters. The island is still privately owned and permission is needed to land there.

At the tiny community of Gribun, the road climbs through high ground. It is open, sheep country, giving way to conifers, which restrict the view as you descend to Loch Scridain. Here the road runs along the loch side to meet the A849. It is 8.5 miles/13km from Gribun. As you proceed up the loch side there is a splendid view to the hills beyond the loch.

From this uninhabited road junction, it is 18 miles/29 km to Fionnphort. For much of the way, the road runs along or close to the coast, moving inland for a relatively straight run just prior to Bunessan into that village, and then another one from there to Fionnphort. There are stores near the head of the loch (and a hotel) at the small community of Pennyghael. The main community on this long peninsula (the Ross of Mull) is at Bunessan, with its car park on the tiny harbour at the head of Loch Na Lathaich.

Driving on this road can be labourious, it is single track and frequently used, involving much pulling over into laybys. Bunessan has a Spar shop, hotel, and toilets on the waterfront. There is petrol/diesel both in Fionnphort and at Ardfenaig, 3 miles/5km nearer Bunessan. Fionnphort is also the home of the Ninth Wave Restaurant, awarded the Restaurant of the Year Award in the Highland and Islands Food and Drinks Awards. [Contact: Bruach Mhor, Fionnphort, Mull, PA66 6BL; Tel: 01681 700757; reservations essential, closed Mondays and normally from Oct-Easter. Dinner only, licence stipulates no children under 12 years old.]

Access to the south side of the Ross of Mull, south west of Loch Buie is limited to two roads plus access to beaches south of Fionnphort (see pages 12-13). At the top of the hill on the Fionnphort road from Bunessan, a turn left goes over to Uisken. There is a beach here, with rocky outcrops in the bay, a welcome place if you are looking for peace and quiet (see also page 12). Another road leaves Pennyghael for Carsaig, another small beach with walks beneath the cliffs and by the shoreline to the east and west.

The Ross of Mull contains much red granite. It was used commercially and most notably in the building of the Albert Memorial in London.

Craignure to Loch Scridain (A849)

From the jetty at Craignure, a left turn takes you away from the coast. Just under 2 miles along the A849, a left turn takes you around Duart Bay to Duart Castle, situated dramatically above the Sound of Mull at Duart Point. The castle is the home of the Chief of the Clan Maclean. It is open to the public and there is also a coffee shop and gift shop. There are extensive views out to sea and if you are on a trip out from Oban, CalMac have a ferry/castle combined ticket with a bus connection from Craignure included. The castle incorporates a tower house and parts date back to the 13th century. Reduced to a ruin after being abandoned by 1751, the site was restored to a dwelling once more in 1912 by Sir Fitzroy Donald Maclean. [Contact: ☎ 01680 812309]

A further 3miles/5km along the A849 brings you to the inner end of Loch Spelve, a sea loch. After a further mile there is a left turn to Lochbuie (see p. 12). The Iona road continues onwards through mountains and along Glen More to reach Loch Scridain. The road from there is described on p.23

ABOVE: Bunessan

BELOW: Fionnphort

ABOVE: The Abbey, Iona

BELOW: The Abbey Church nave

Iona

Upon reaching Fionnphort, there is roadside parking (car park fee) for the ferry to Iona. It is next to the ferry terminal (CalMac). There are toilets here and on the ferry, but you pay to use one at the terminal. It only takes 10 minutes to cross to Baile Mor (usually referred to as The Village) and you can see both it and the abbey before you leave. There is a Spar shop near the terminal and another on Iona where there are also a general store, bookshop, a gallery. Heritage Centre and several craft shops.

A long line of cottages faces you as you cross to Iona, each one with a garden stretching down towards the foreshore. Upon arrival, pass these and turn right by the impressive remains of an early 13th century Nunnery. The interior is laid out as a garden. Enough of the buildings survive to give you a good idea of what it looked like when complete. In fact it is one of the best remains of a medieval nunnery in Britain and the best in Scotland.

Passing this by, you soon reach the tall and slender Maclean's Cross, close to the Argyll Hotel (open to visitors for refreshments). The cross (over 9ft / 3m high) is one of only three of well over 300 to survive the Reformation. The style of a cross head with a circle of stone imposed upon it (called disc-headed) apparently originated here. However Henry VIII's Reformation saw the flowering of culture and the heart of Scottish Christianity scattered to the four winds. The two other crosses stand outside the abbey (now parish) church, although one is strictly a replica, its original now kept safely indoors.

Maclean's Cross, dated to c.1500 by Historic Scotland, stands on a lane which passes the bookshop and a craft shop and runs up to the north of the island beyond the abbey, which is a little north of the hotel. Historic Scotland takes care of the complex. Once inside the churchyard, you can visit the12th century Oran's Chapel and see the ancient graves of 48 Scottish kings, 4 Irish kings and 8 Norwegian and French. Macbeth lies here but all the gravestones have lost their inscriptions and more is the pity. Also here rests John Smith, Leader of the Labour Party, who died in 1994.

The original monastery here was founded by Columba in AD 563 and became an important centre of learning. However the Vikings began to attack it from AD 794 and it was abandoned in AD 849. Benedictine nuns established a convent here in c.1208, following the building of the current abbey five years earlier. Although it lost its roof, it was not pillaged for stone. Even older than the church is St Martin's Cross outside the west front which dates from the 9th century. Its intricate carving is worth stopping to examine.

The first thing that strikes you on entering the church is its small size, but it is largely complete. In 1874, the 8th Duke of Argyll commissioned stabilisation repairs, but it remained roofless, its floors grass covered. In 1899, the year before the Duke died at Inverary castle, he gave the abbey site to the Iona Catholic Trust. In 1902, restoration began and although the first service was in 1905, it was 1910 before the inaugural service (26/6/1910).

The final part of the redevelopment started in the Depression, when out-of-work craftsmen from Glasgow built the Cloister. The rest of the monastery took until 1965 to complete. In the south transept are the fine, recumbent figures of the 8th Duke (George Douglas Campbell) and his third wife Ina, carved in marble. The nave is unusual, having a step down below the tower. Off to the left (north side) are the cloisters and the abbey museum.

If time permits, you can walk up the road (turn right) on leaving the churchyard. This takes you past the abbey shop and on to the north of the island, with a path extending the last bit to the coast. Returning to the jetty, a road goes to the right passed the Spar shop and the Finlay Ross store. Continue on for a short distance to where the road turns right and follow this to the west coast, about a mile away. Here is the golf course (free) and a track running a little over a mile down to the south coast at Port an Fhir-bhreige. Just to the left here (as you face the sea) is Port na Curaich where Columba is believed to have landed.

Iona: A Special Place

Small islands always seem to share a similar and unique characteristic, but here there seems to be a special quality to it. Surely it is subjective; however, it always seems to be there. Dr Johnson, on his visit in October 1773 wandered around the abbey, its buildings and church all then in ruins. It was to remain so for well over a century. None the less, both he and James Boswell, his companion and biographer, felt some sort of special atmosphere on Iona. He said 'That man is little to be envied…whose piety would not grow warmer among the ruins of Iona'.

Maybe that is it: seeing the impressive and so very ancient crosses; the compact abbey church; even its cloisters, reconstructed comparatively recently; the knowledge of so much history encompassing the arrival of Columba in AD 563; the resting place of perhaps 60 kings etc imbues one with a sense that this place is so very special. Yet it does so in such a passive way.

Whether your devotion is stirred or just your sense of history, this simple place somehow creates a sense of warmth; a compellingness to go there and maybe go back again; a feeling of wellbeing of having done it.

ABOVE: Abbey Cloisters

BELOW: The tomb of the 8th Duke of Argyll

GEORGE DOVGLAS
VIII DVKE OF ARGYLL
1823 [illegible] 1900

Staffa

Staffa is well known for being the site of Fingal's Cave, perhaps the best known sea-cave in Britain. Uninhabited since at least Victorian times, Staffa lies 6 miles/9.5 km north of Iona and the same distance from the nearest point of Mull. It is 54 miles/87km west of Oban. It is about 1.5 miles/2 km in circumference and rises to a height of just under 150 ft/46m. It is famous for its six-sided columnar basalt formations.

Fingal's Cave is the largest of several caves which pierce the basalt rock. It is 227 ft/69m long, 42 ft/13m wide and about 60 ft/18m high. There is a stairway up onto the flat top of the cliffs at Clamshell Cave and a 300 yard/274m causeway from the landing point to Fingal's Cave along the tops of the basalt columns, similar to Giants Causeway, in Northern Ireland. There are no facilities ashore.

The island is now owned by the National Trust for Scotland [Contact: ☎ 01463 232034] and was declared a National Nature Reserve in 2001. It has a large seabird population, with dolphins, porpoises and sometimes a whale to be observed nearby. The island is fertile and once supported a couple of crofts. Staffa is open daily, but boat trips tend to be seasonal.

Getting There

Turus Mara ☎ Freephone 08000 858786; e: info@turusmara.com
From Iona, C. Kirkpatrick ☎ 01681 700358; e: iolare@staffatrips.co.uk
Staffa Tours ☎ 07732 912370 www.staffatours.com

ABOVE: Iona: The Village with the Nunnery on the left and the Argyll Hotel on the right

BELOW: The Village from the jetty

ABOVE: Iona: The Village

LEFT: Staffa basalt columns RIGHT: Fingal's Cave , Staffa / Photos: Mark Titterton

Further Information

Tobermory Tourist Information

plus accommodation, boat and wildlife trips etc

☎ 01688 302875/ 301268/ 07812 543190

Calmac: Craignure ☎ 01680 812343

Oban ☎ 01631 566688

Buses; Traveline ☎ 0871 200 2233

Hospital

Dunaros, Salen: ☎ 01680 300392;

Craignure Cottage Hospital: ☎ as Dunaros

Doctor ☎ 01688 302013

Dentist ☎ 01688 302105

Police Station ☎ 01688 302016

Published by

Guidelines Books & Sales

11 Belmont Road, Ipstones, Stoke on Trent ST10 2JN

☎ 07971 990649 email: author.porter@gmail.com

ISBN 978-1-84306-554-8

Printed by Berforts Information Press Ltd, Eynsham, Oxford

Disclaimer

While every care has been taken to ensure that the information in this book is as accurate as possible at the time of publication, the publisher accepts no responsibility for any loss, injury or inconvenience etc sustained by anyone using this book.

Front Cover: Tobermory